'Beautifully written and illustrated . . . will resonate with any young person who has ever felt a build up of emotion.'

Andrew Cowley, author of *The Wellbeing Toolkit* and *The Wellbeing Curriculum*.

The Red String

Using a red string as a metaphor for the energy of strong feelings, this beautifully written storybook is a journey of the physical sensations of anger as it runs through the character's body – making them want to punch as it gets into their arms, kick and stomp as it travels down their legs and scream out hateful things as it wraps itself around their heart.

Full of relatable and easy to understand scenarios, *The Red String*:

- has a gender-neutral central character
- helps children to identify powerful feelings like anger and recognise their possible effects
- introduces the strategy of allowing the energy of strong feelings to 'dance' in our body, instead of letting them control our thoughts and behaviour
- enables children to begin to accept strong feelings such as anger, without shame or judgment
- ends with a mindful reflection, to help children explore and be with their feelings.

Strong feelings can be overwhelming and consuming. This book is essential reading for teachers, parents, or anyone working with young people who wishes to help children understand, embrace and cope with powerful feelings such as anger, in a healthy way.

Anita Kate Garai is a teacher, writer and mindful wellbeing consultant.

The Red String

Exploring the Energy of Anger and Other Strong Emotions

Anita Kate Garai

Illustrated by Pip Williams

Routledge
Taylor & Francis Group

LONDON AND NEW YORK

Cover illustration credit: © Pip Williams

Logo and 'bubbles' design © 2022 Liz Tui Morris, www.bolster.co.nz

First published 2023

by Routledge

4 Park Square, Milton Park, Abingdon, Oxon OX14 4RN

and by Routledge

605 Third Avenue, New York, NY 10158

Routledge is an imprint of the Taylor & Francis Group, an informa business

© 2023 Anita Kate Garai

Illustrations © 2022 Pip Williams

British Library Cataloguing-in-Publication Data
A catalogue record for this book is available from the British Library

Library of Congress Cataloging-in-Publication Data
Names: Garai, Anita Kate, author. | Williams, Pip (Illustrator), illustrator.
Title: The red string : exploring the energy of anger and other strong emotions / Anita Kate Garai ; illustrated by Pip Williams.
Description: Milton Park, Abingdon, Oxon ; New York, NY : Routledge, 2022.
Identifiers: LCCN 2021051866 (print) | LCCN 2021051867 (ebook) | ISBN 9781032233987 (paperback) | ISBN 9781003280156 (ebook)
Subjects: LCSH: Anger in children—Juvenile literature. | Emotions in children—Juvenile literature.
Classification: LCC BF723.A4 G37 2022 (print) | LCC BF723.A4 (ebook) | DDC 155.4/1247—dc23/eng/20220125
LC record available at https://lccn.loc.gov/2021051866
LC ebookrecord available at https://lccn.loc.gov/2021051867

ISBN: 978-1-032-23398-7 (pbk)

ISBN: 978-1-003-28015-6 (ebk)

DOI: 10.4324/9781003280156

Typeset in Londrina

by Apex CoVantage, LLC

For Angelina. Thank you for the inspiration.

I have some red string that lives in my toes.   How it got itself there, nobody knows.

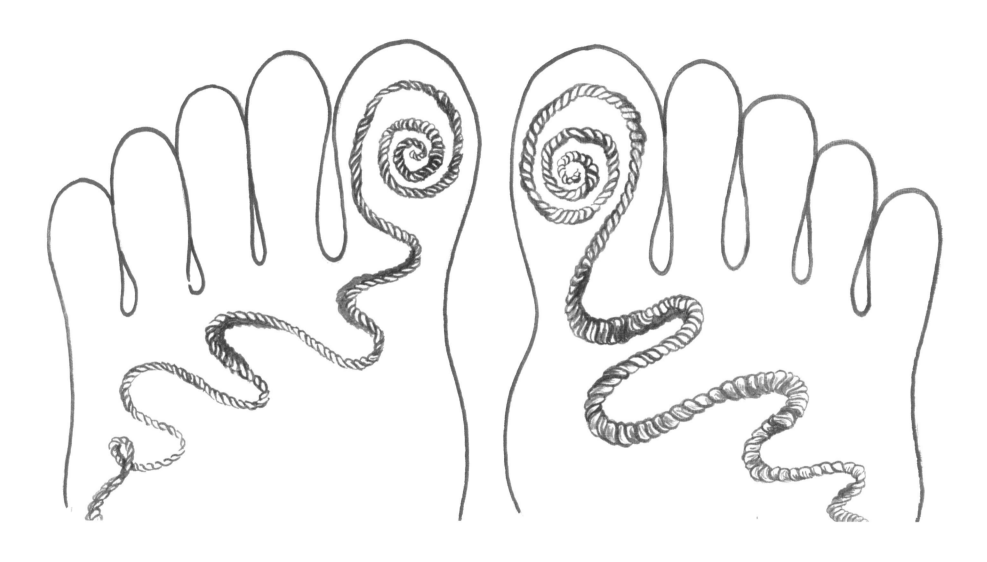

It's my little secret,

'till it starts to move,

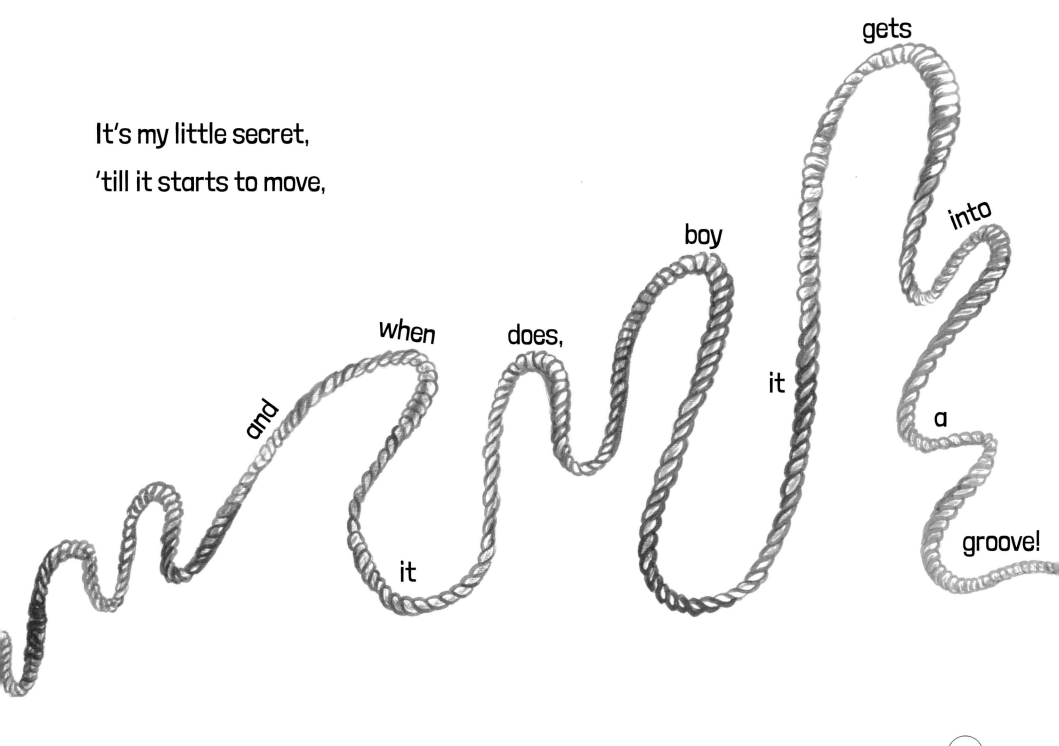

and when it does, boy it gets into a groove!

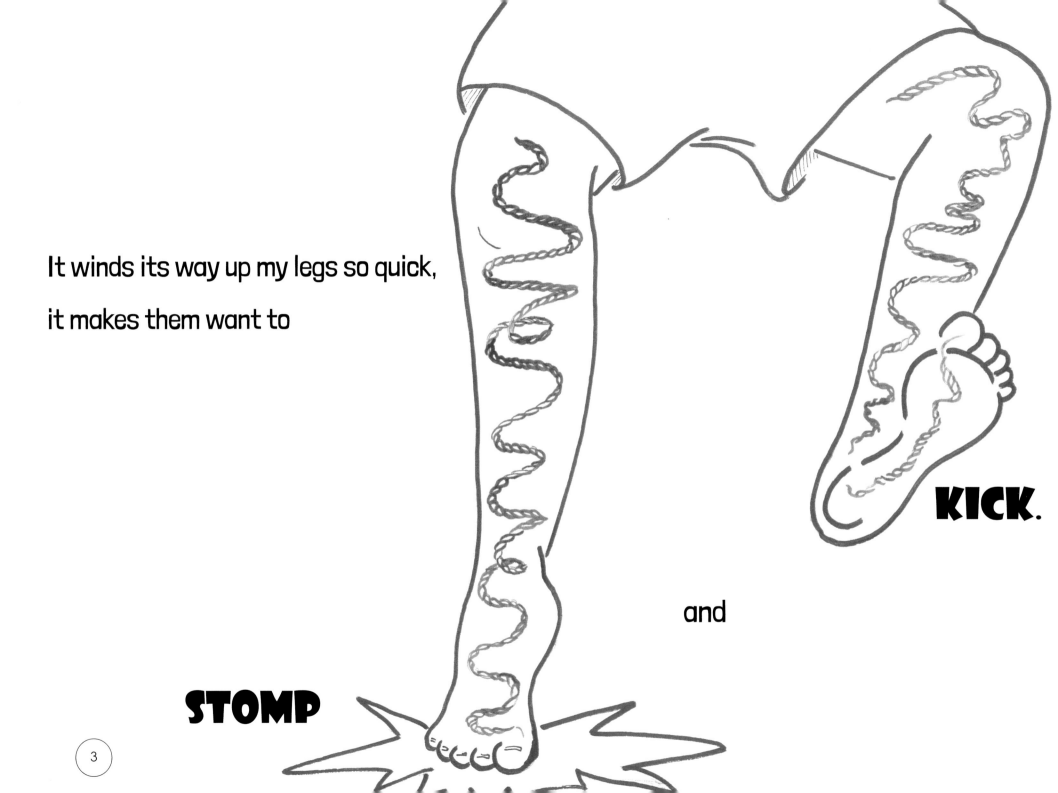

It winds its way up my legs so quick,
it makes them want to

KICK.

and

STOMP

When it gets to my belly it can hurt a lot

as it ties itself up into a **big**, red knot.

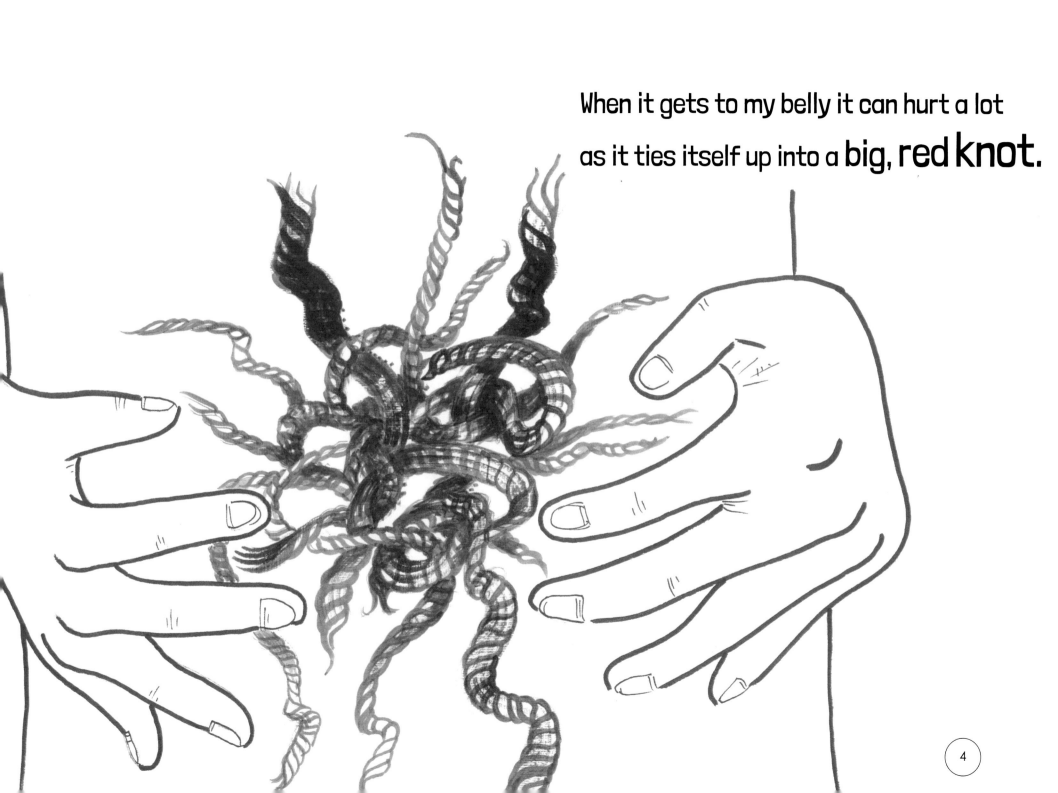

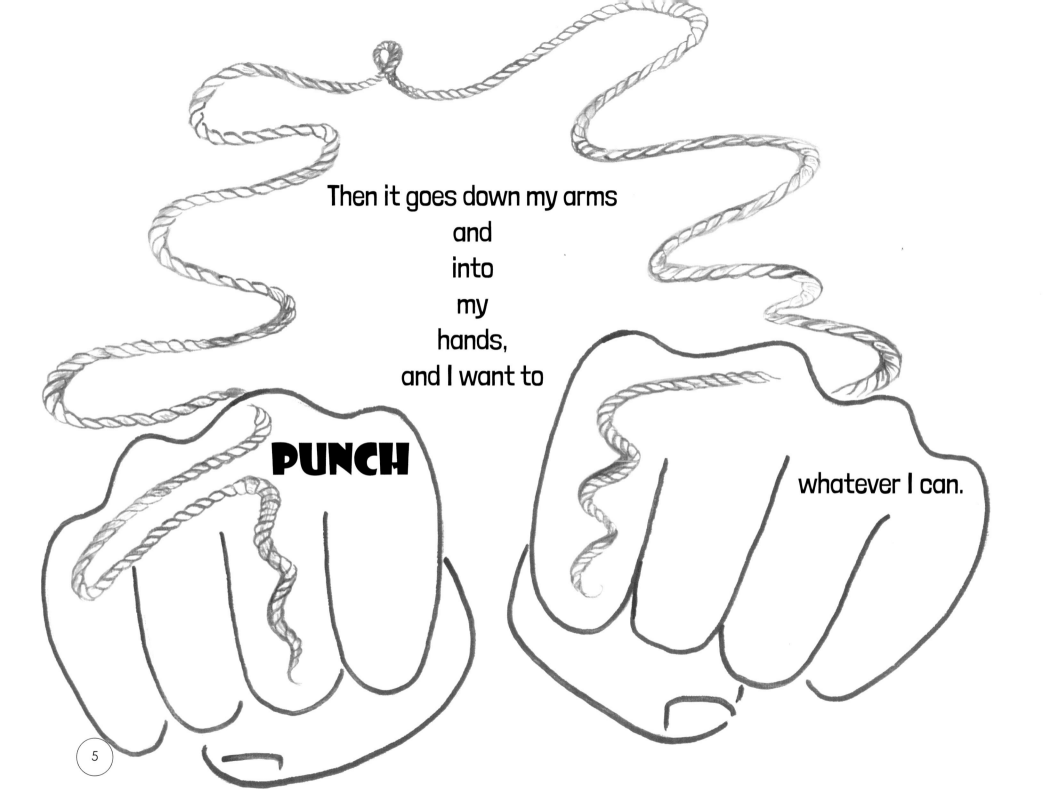

Then it goes down my arms
and
into
my
hands,
and I want to

PUNCH

whatever I can.

Sometimes it travels all over my skin

and makes me turn red,

both outside

and in.

If it finds the path all the way up to my head,

I can say awful things, like

'I WISH YOU WERE DEAD!'

7

Sometimes it even gets

stuck in my hair

by which time,

if I make someone cry,

I don't care.

'Cos the thing is, by then it has torn me apart

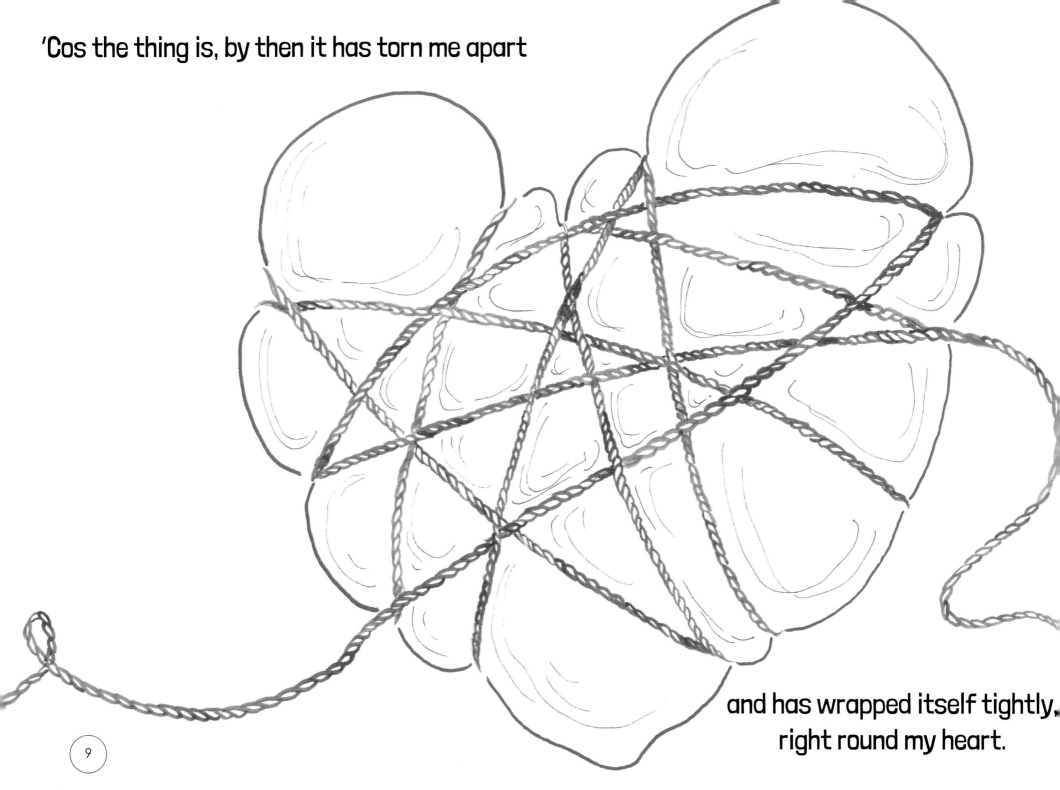

and has wrapped itself tightly,
right round my heart.

When it gets to that point, there is really no way that I can feel love,

only **hate** has a say

And then I might shout

or stomp

or have fits

or rip my best toy

into

tiny

little

bits.

11

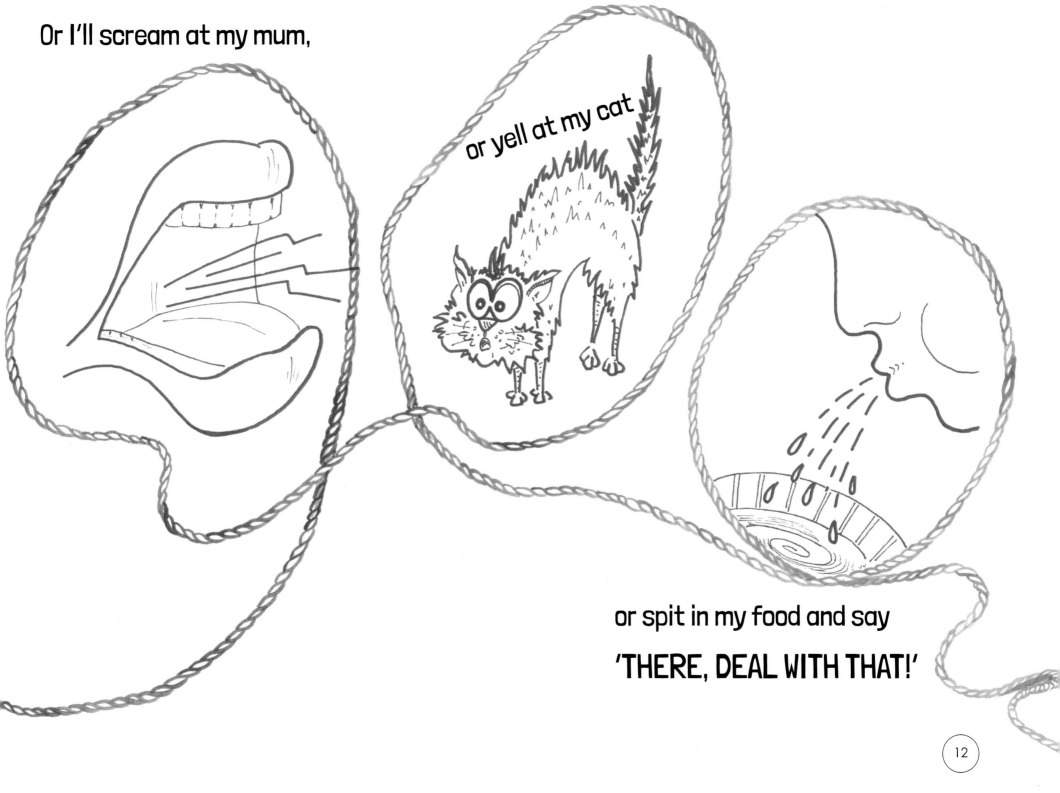

Or I'll scream at my mum,

or yell at my cat

or spit in my food and say

'THERE, DEAL WITH THAT!'

12

Or I'll just hold my breath till my lips turn blue,

'cos I don't know what else there is I can do.

And then I remember what Sam used to say.

He said, "Breathe in and out really slowly and stay

as still as you can,

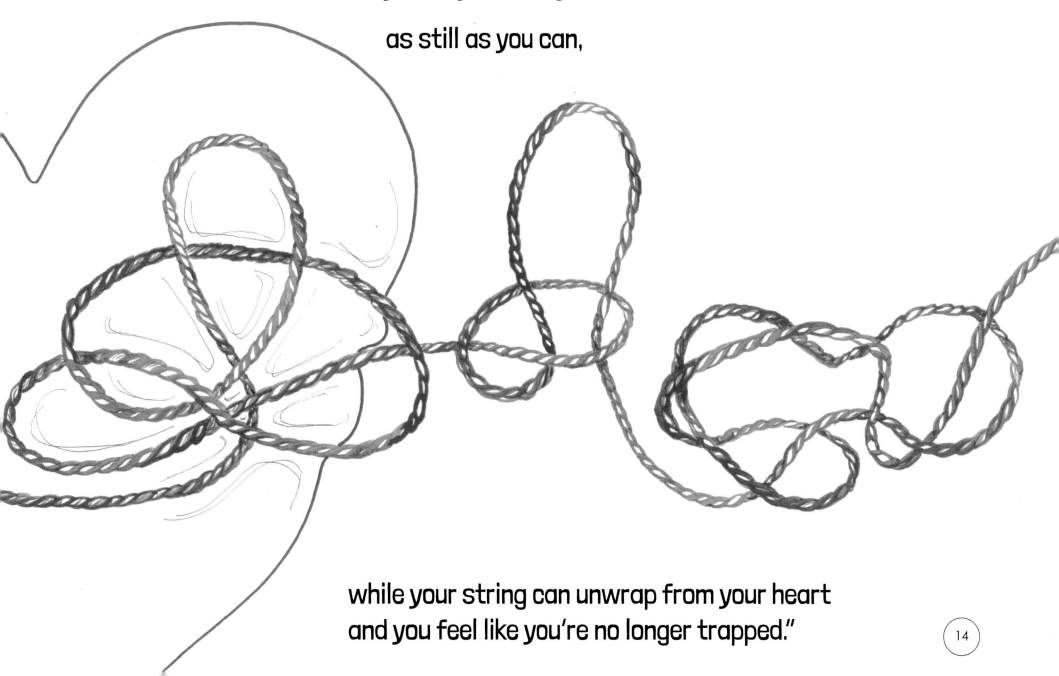

while your string can unwrap from your heart
and you feel like you're no longer trapped."

14

So I stop

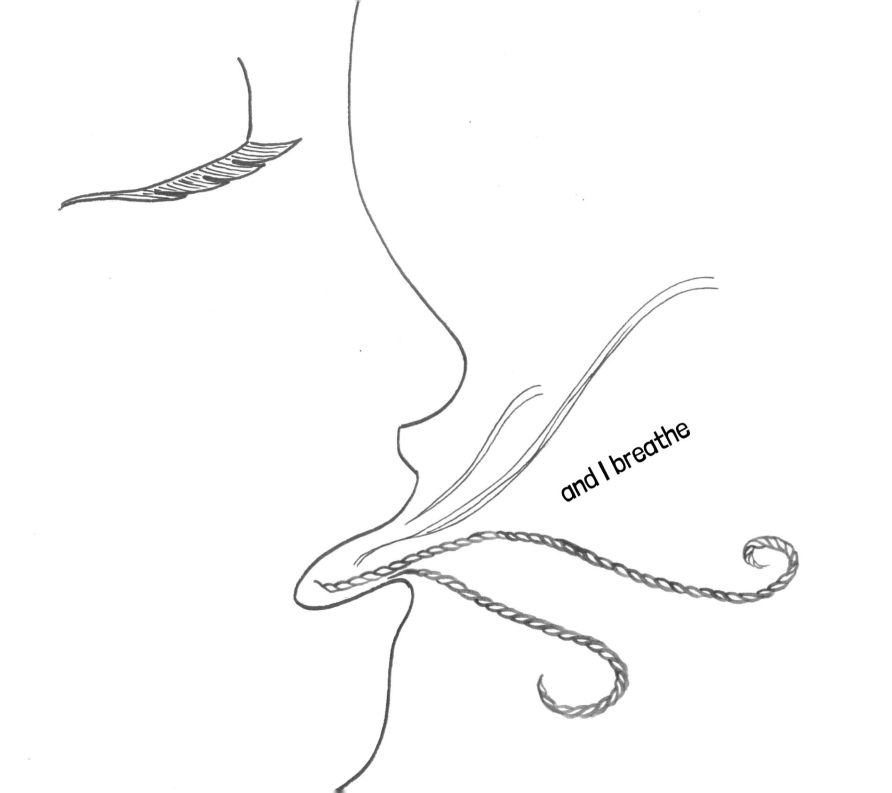

and I breathe

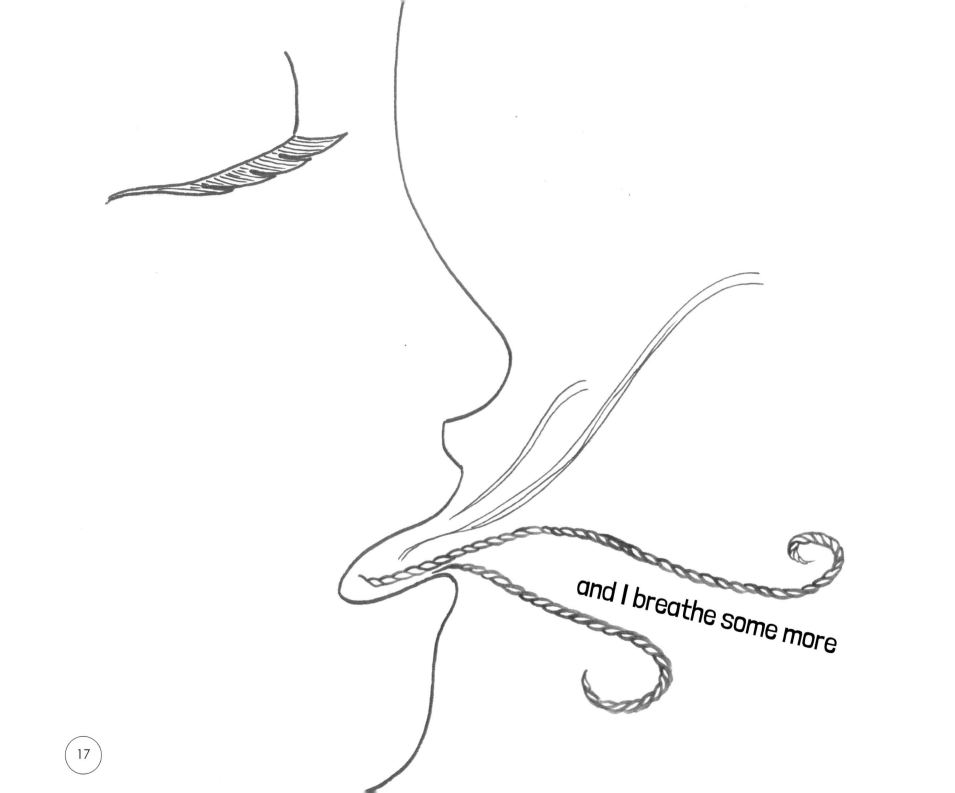

and I breathe some more

and I feel my feet firmly flat on the floor.

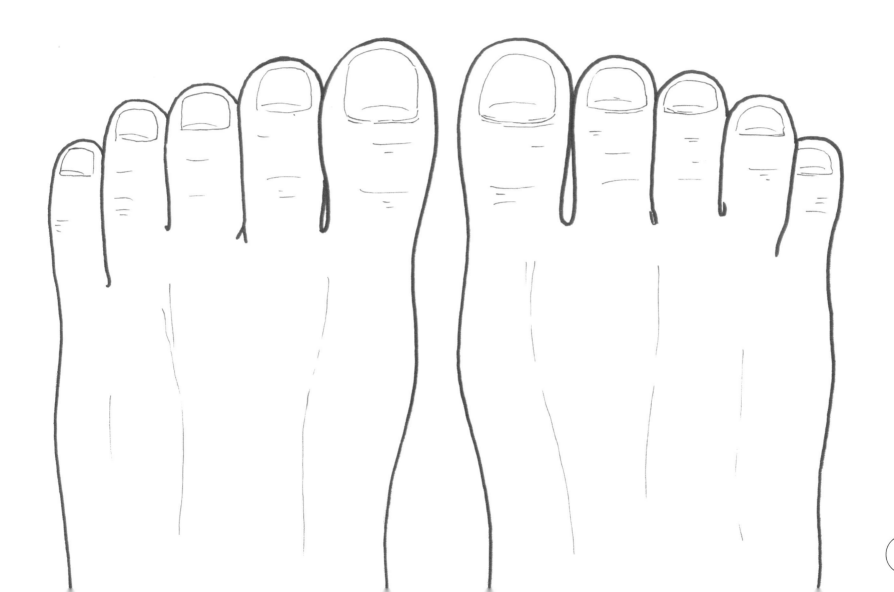

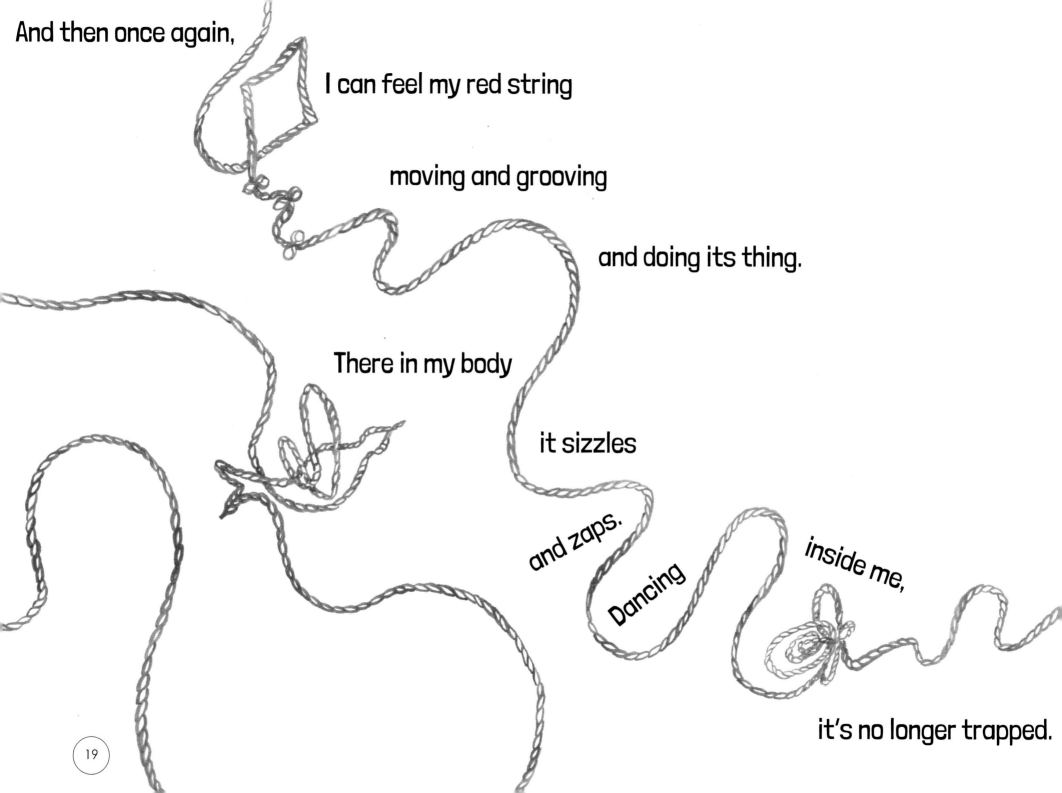

And then once again,

I can feel my red string

moving and grooving

and doing its thing.

There in my body

it sizzles

and zaps.

Dancing

inside me,

it's no longer trapped.

As my red string keeps moving

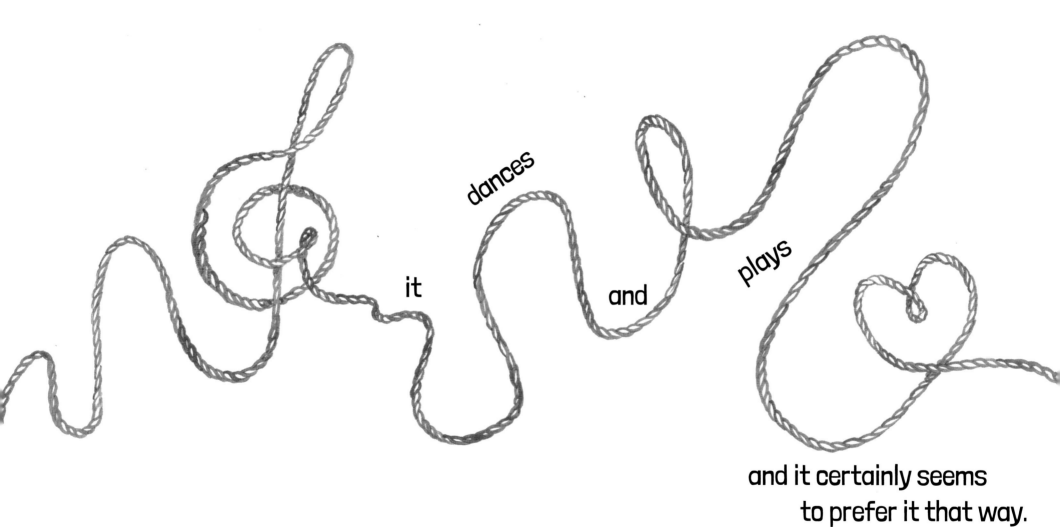

it dances and plays

and it certainly seems
to prefer it that way.

And then when it's ready it starts to retreat,

finding its way

back

into

my

feet.

And then it goes . . .

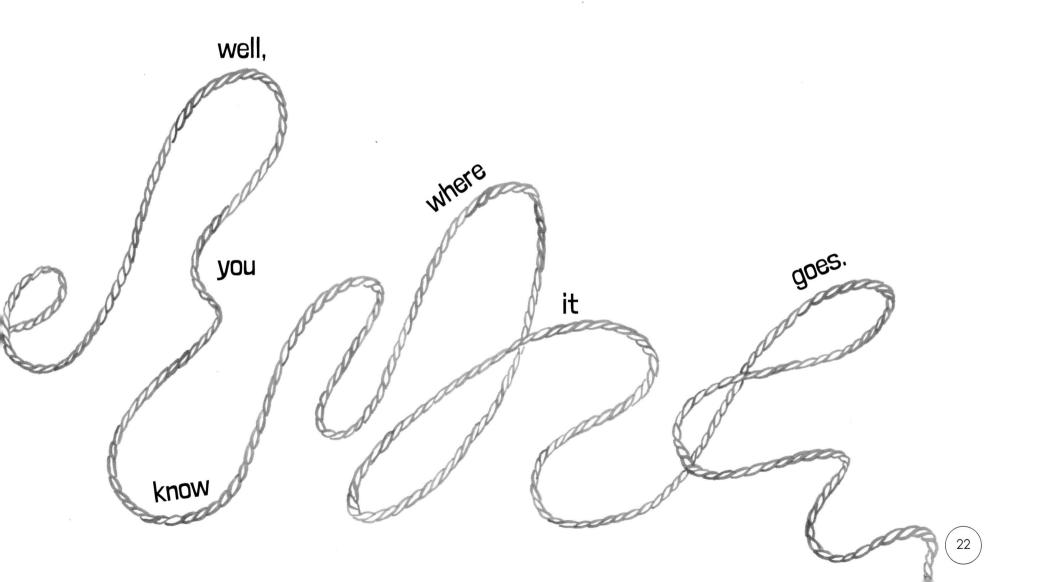

well,

you

know

where

it

goes.

That's right!

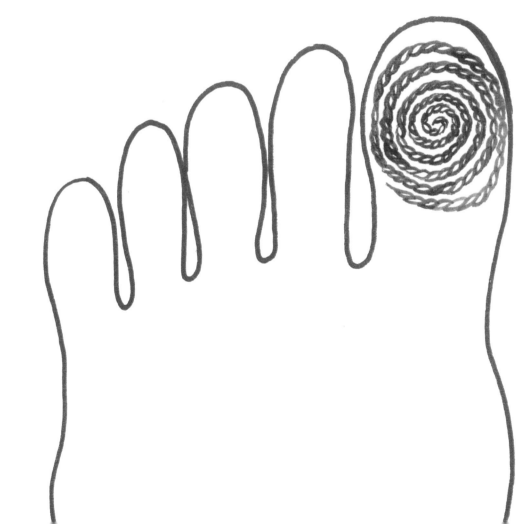

It finally goes back to my toes.

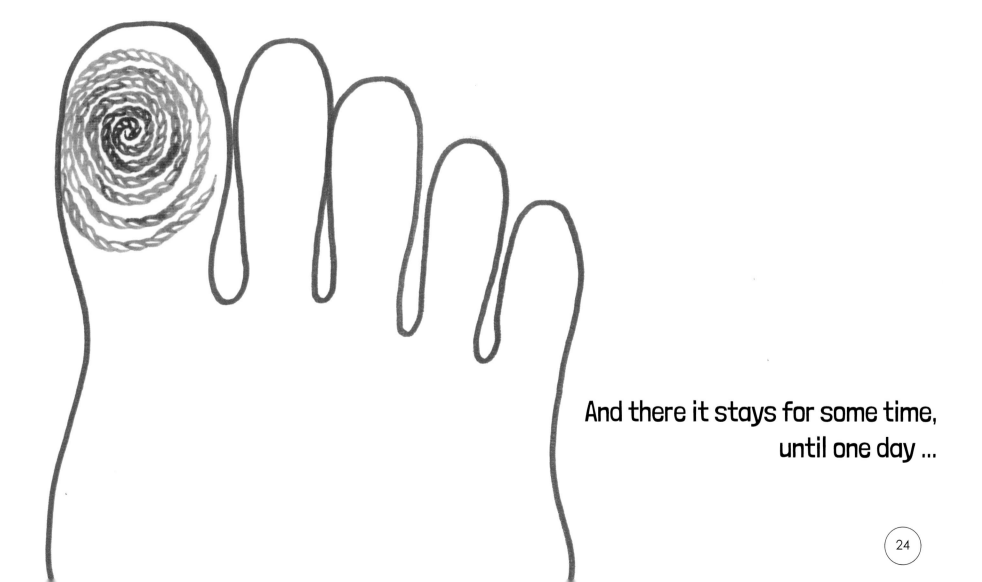

And there it stays for some time,
until one day ...

my string once again   comes out to play.

Reflection

The red string has a lot of energy and movement. The narrator can feel it in different parts of their body. When you have a strong emotion, can you feel it in your body? Whereabouts? If it moves around, what kind of movements does it make? Is yours like a red string too, or is it something else? As you reflect on these questions, notice any feelings in your body right now.

Does the feeling have a colour?

Does the feeling have a shape?

Does the feeling have a movement?

Does the feeling have a sound?

More reflections, activities and explorations are available in *Being With Our Feelings, – A Mindful Approach to Wellbeing for Children: A Teaching Toolkit* by Anita Kate Garai (Routledge, 2022).

Printed in the UK by Severn, Gloucester on responsibly sourced paper